Come my young master and mistress too,
Fairings in plenty, and all for you!
Apples and pears, Juicy and mellow,
Honey-sweet plums, Purple and yellow,
Candies and sweets, Cakes made of honey,
Lasses and lads, Out with your money!

Come my young master and mistress too,
Fairings in plenty, and all for you!
Ribbons of green, Orange and blue, miss,
Kerchiefs of silk, Dainty as you, miss,
Brooches and beads, Which will you buy, sir?
Lockets and rings, Maidens are shy, sir.

Come my young master and mistress too,
Fairings in plenty,
Fairings in plenty,
Fairings in plenty,
and all for you!

By   Helen Taylor
Enoch and Sons.

VICTORIAN

FAIRINGS

AND THEIR

VALUES

VICTORIAN FAIRINGS AND THEIR VALUES

First Published June 1975

Copyright ©

LYLE PUBLICATIONS

glenmayne galashiels Selkirkshire Scotland

Printed by MORRISON & GIBB LTD   P. O. Box 44
Tanfield Edinburgh

ACKNOWLEDGEMENTS

The publishers wish to acknowledge and thank the following for their kind help and assistance in the production of this volume: The Marquis of Bristol; Caroline Treffgarne; Mrs. F. Shephard; Mr. & Mrs. E. Broad; Mrs. R. T. Gardner; Mrs. D. Charles; Mr. M. R. Davies; Walter Hayes; Sheila Wilson; Victoria Scott; David MacWilliams; Mr. & Mrs. A. Leeds; Christie's: Phillips. And a special thanks to JOHN HALL, PAUL VINEY and DAVID MORRIS without whose help this book would not have been possible.

Introduction

MR. MICAWBER

Most of us have at one time or another visited the Fair, to return home highly delighted with some small token won at one of the stalls — Perhaps the hoopla, or even the coconut shying. Whichever stall it was that benefited from our patronage mattered little compared to the joy we felt at gaining a prize which, more often than not, was a very cheaplike dog, cat or even human figure of plaster and worth only a few pence.

Had we lived in the late 19th century, we would more than likely have come home the proud owner of a little china figure which is now referred to as a 'fairing'. These fairings were mostly about 4ins high and 2¼ins in width and mounted on rectangular bases. Each one, and there were over 400 different varieties, depicted an amusing scene either of risque courtship and marriage, or of politics, war, children, and sometimes animals behaving as children. Most fairings bore a caption and all were made of china. The early examples (1860/1870) were generally slightly larger and of better quality than later figures. Those of 1870/1880 show definite signs of mass production, being more clumsily moulded and with flat bases. The colouring on these was of an inferior quality in

'Dick Whittington'. A typically English theme.

comparison with the earlier models. After 1890 the colours used were even more garish and it was at this time that gilding on the base was added. These fairings were generally lighter in weight.

When we dwell on the subject of fairings we automatically think of them as typically English, and it often comes as rather a surprise to learn that they were manufactured mostly in Germany by Conte and Boehme of Pössneck. It would seem that this firm had perfected cheap mass production methods to such a level that British manufacturers could not compete at all.

It is a strange fact that there is very little contemporaneous information available about fairings, possibly because they were regarded then as contemptuously as plaster figures are today, but there is now a growing tendency to collect these interesting and delightful ornaments. Interest now is worldwide, and collectors from all over the globe show great interest in the specialised auction sales held by both Christies and Phillips of London who each have many sales throughout the year.

In this publication I have given the current values of fairings from prices taken over the past fifteen months. These tend to fluctuate somewhat in sympathy with the state of the economy generally, but increases have been noted, particularly with the cheaper fairings, during the early part of 1975 and the outlook is favourable. It cannot be too strongly emphasised that the prices given are for perfect specimens only. For example, one very rare fairing entitled 'To Epsom' fetched 1,400

'To Epsom'

guineas in February 1974 at Christie's of London. A similar example with the same caption dropped to £720 at the next auction, the reason for this being that the figure was minus a head.

It will be noticed that there is frequently more than one caption for the same fairing. For example, one entitled 'Dangerous Encounter' (two girls riding boneshaker bicycles) sometimes appears as 'Girls of the Period'. There are also examples of the same fairing 'Tug of War' with a French caption 'La Bataille'. 'Spoils of War' appears again as 'La Victoire' and 'Favourable Opportunity' with a German caption 'Bitte mein Fraulein'. There is

also 'Oysters Sir' and a caption 'Oesteers Mynheer'. These are only a few named examples to illustrate the different varieties.

There are also entirely different fairings showing the same caption. 'Awkward Interruption', showing a man getting out of bed with a cat on his back, is also shown as a man holding a maid's hand whilst his wife walks in. These we have listed for convenience of valuation as two different pieces.

Conte and Boehme of Pössneck also produced uncaptioned fairings which were intended primarily for sale in shops, rather than as fairground prizes. Although some of these are replicas of the captioned variety, they have been shown in a different part of the book in order to avoid possible confusion. Throughout the period, the manufacturers produced decorated china boxes and match strikers. Some were captioned and the figures on the lids were identical to those on fairings and clearly, these too, were included for the same markets.

The manufacturers have obviously borrowed many of their ideas for fairings from such printed materials as sheet music covers. Two, entitled 'Pluck' and 'The Decided Smash' are copies from the cover of a popular song sheet of the time called 'Full Cry Gallop'. In the case of 'Slack' and 'How's

11

English neutrality attending the sick and the wounded.

Business', these are very good copies of each side of a Staffordshire mug. 'Champagne Charlie is my name' represents George Leybourne making popular the song 'Champagne Charlie' in the 1860s. There are also a few scenes of the Franco-Prussian War which include 'English Neutrality attending the Sick and Wounded'. (As illustrated above).

We hope that the reader will derive some enjoyment and interest from this publication and gain some insight into the humour that went into the manufacture of these very delightful china ornaments. They were made for the purpose of giving pleasure to the masses who thronged to the Fairs, and part of the pleasure of their ownership springs from the high possibility that each was won and given in a spirit of fun and affection.

MARGARET ANDERSON

The prices given in this publication represent the current market values of fairings at the time of going to press, having been computed from auction and retail sales figures gathered throughout Great Britain.

It will be seen that a few of the higher-priced fairings have been valued somewhat below the figures obtained at auction in 1973. In general, however, prices show a steady upward trend, and the indications are that this will continue.

After   £75

After Marriage   £30

After Marriage
Sold with 'Before Marriage'   £150

After the Ball   £75

After the Race 1875   £25

Alone at Last   £30

After You My Dear Alphonso   £120

Am I Right, Or Any Other Man   £40

All Over (small)   £300

An Awkward Interruption   £60

An Awkward Interruption £45

An Awkward Interruption £30

Angels Whisper, The £30

An Awkward Interruption £40 Animated Spirits £600

Animated Spirits
A tipsy man with two girls.
Very rare and unrecorded at auction
Price subject to negotiation but unlikely to be less than   **£400**

Announcement   **£30**

Any Flags Ma'am   **£45**

Anti Vivisectors   **£16**

Anxious To Study   **£55**

Any Lights Sir?   **£70**
Also captioned 'Match Sir?'

Attack   £35

Attentive Maid, The   £150

 B

Babes in the Wood, The   £450

Baby   £30

Baby's First Step   £32

Before £200

Baby's First Step £40

Badervergnugen

Depicts a lady in a mud bath assisted by a maid. Very rare. At least £600

Bataille, La £35
(Also Captioned 'Tug of War')

Baumwolle oder Seide

Very rare and unrecorded at auction. Price subject to negotiation but unlikely to be less than £600

Before Darwin £5

Before Marriage £60

18

Before Marriage £150

Man and woman embracing on a sofa.

Be good and if You Can't Be Good Be Careful. £30

Benoni and Leila £25

Between Two Stools You Fall To The Ground. £225

Beware of a Collision £380

Bishop of Salford £20

Bitte Mein Fraulein £70
Same as 'Favourable Opportunity'

Girl alighting from carriage showing her ankles whilst a coachman watches.

Broken Hoop, The £120	By Golly I am in Luck £40

By Appointment The First of April   £240

Cabin Baggage £6

Can Can £350

Campbell £20

Can Can £450

Can Can £300

Can Can £350

Can You Do This Grandma? £220

A Cat A Cat £28

Carnarvon to Liverpool £10

A Cat, A Cat £40

Caught £85

Caught In the Act   £220

Charles Dickens   £10

Chaste Joseph, The

Very rare and unrecorded at auction. Price subject to negotiation but unlikely to be less than   **£600**

A woman with one breast exposed is drawing a man's hand towards her. He screens his gaze with his other hand.

Checkmate   £180

Champagne Charlie is My Name   £140

Checkmate   £180

Children's Meeting £26

Cold Hands, Cold Feet (Fake caption) £16

Child's Prayer £30

Come Along these Flowers Don't Smell Very Good £70

Cinderella £10

Come Away Do £700

Come Pussie Come
A couple about to get into bed with
a cat.   £25

Coming Home From the Seaside £250

Consommation
Very rare and unrecorded at auction.
Price subject to negotiation but un-
likely to be less than   **£600**
A man blessing a young woman and
man kneeling in front of him.

Constitutional
Figure of a man reading a paper **£50**

Cousin and Cousine   **£95**

Cupid's Watching   **£200**

Cupid's Watching   **£200**

Copper Sir?, A   **£45**

Curtain Lecture   **£16**

Daily News Sir £70

Daily Telegraph, The
Boy holding newspaper (match-striker)
£70

Dangerous £380

Dangerous Encounter £350

Decided Smash, The £40

Defeat £35

Delights of Matrimony, The £25

Did You Call Sir? £400

Der Letze Loscht das Licht Aus £12

Did You Ring Sir? £240

Dick Whittington and His Cat £8

Die Folgen Spater Heimkehr £14

Difficult Problem, A £8

Doctor, The £11

Difficult Problem, A £15

Dolphus Won't Tell Papa. £500

Disagreeable Surprise

A man seated on the ground is hit by another man as a woman leans out of a window and hits him with a saucepan. £294

Don't Awake the Baby £100

Don't You Like the Change? £920

Doubtful Case, A £200

Don't You Wish You May Get It? £20

Drummer Boy (Caption added). £20

 E

Early Bird Catches the Worm, The
Man relieving himself at a fence with
an alert chicken studying him £70
Eastern Lovers £15

Eighty Strokes of the Pulse in the
Minute £460

Elizabeth and Henry Vlll £20

Enfin Seule (see Alone At Last)
Maid peering through a keyhole £35

Engaged £20

English Neutrality 1890 Attending the Wounded £220

English Neutrality 1890 Attending the Sick £220

Evening Prayer £21

English Neutrality 1890 Attending the Sick and Wounded £350

Every Vehicle Driven by a Horse, Mule or Ass £400

Fair Play Boys   £450

Fast Asleep   £25

Family Cares   £12

Favourable Opportunity   £60

Fast Asleep   £12

Feeling Dizzy   £20

31

Fine Hairs £200

First Pray £30

Fishmonger, The £400
Figure of a Fishmonger in his stall

First Caresses £450

First Temptation £12 **Fishwives** £12

Five O'Clock Tea   £40

Folgen Spater Heimkehr   £40
(Also captioned 'Returning at One O'Clock in the Morning')

For Heavens Sake Maria Give us a Rest
  £45

Five O' Clock Tea   £40

Free and Independent Electors   £420

Flower Seller, The   £25

Fresh Chestnuts, Sir   £50

Friend in Need is a Friend Indeed

A child on a chamberpot putting one under another child. £20

Fresh Morning, A £70

Funny Story, A £40

 G

Game of Patience £20

Gentlemen of the Jury £30

Girls of the Period, The £350

Girl Wanted £5

Girl Sitting Before a Door.

God Save the Queen £55

Go Away Mamma I Am Busy £85

Going Going Gone £50

God Bless Our Home £25

Going to the Ball £150

Good Dog (Match Striker, Caption added) **£15**

Good Friends
Dog and Cat Playing on a Sofa. **£60**

Good Templars **£45**

Goodnight **£16**

Good Templars **£60**
(Also Captioned 'Hark Tom')

Grandma Grandpa **£20**

Grandmamma £10

Grandpapa £10

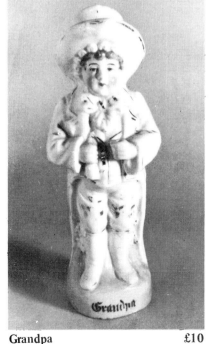

Grandpa £10

Grandpapa £10

Guardian Angel, The £50
Also Captioned 'Our First Efforts Are
Not in Vain'.

Gravelotte £290

Happily Solved £15

(Happy Father) What Two? Yes Sir.
Two Little Beauties!!! £20

(Happy Father) What Two? Yes Sir.
Two Little Beauties!!!   £40

Hark Jo Somebody's Coming   £60

Hark Tom Somebody's Coming   £60

(Happy Father) What Two? Yes Sir.
Two Little Beauties!!!   £200

Harriet Beecher Stowe   £10

(Happy Father) What Two? Yes Sir.
Two Little Beauties!!!   £45

He Don't Like His Pants   £220

Her First Ball   £65

His First Pair   £45

Highland Fling   £25

His First Pair   £28

His First Love Letter   £35

Hit Him Hard   £340

Home From the Club He Fears the Storm £100

Home Sweet Home
Girl painting a landscape with youth admiring it £420

How Bridget Served the Tomatoes Undressed £580

How Happy Could I Be with Either £160

How Quietly They Repose £70

How's Business? £200

How's Your Poor Feet? £480

Hst! My Dolls Sleep   £200

Hunting the Slipper   £50

I Agree With You   £15

I Am Going A-Milking Sir, She Said
   £50

I Am Off With Him   £10

I Am Off With Him   £10

I Am Starting For a Long Journey £10

I Beg Your Pardon   £68

I Am Starting For a Long Journey
                                       £10

Ich Bin Ein Zweiter Salome   £20

43

If Old Age Could (small)   £200
                (large)   £300

I Have Had My Bath, Now Its Your Turn   £25

If You Please Sir   £200

I'm First Sir   £40

If Youth Knew (small)   £250
              (large)   £350

In Chancery   £300

Is't You Barley £15   It's Only Mustache £420

It's A Shame to Take the Money £100   I Will Never Take You Again £5

I Will Warm You £320
(Also captioned 'Quiet Interruption')

I Wish I was a Fish £18

Jealous Wife £47

Just as it Should Be £250

Jenny Jones and Ned Morgan £10

Just in Time £230
(Also captioned 'Come At Once')

Je T'aime Tint £137

46

Kiss Me Quick   £25

Kiss Me Quick   £375

King John   £15

Kiss Me Quick   £25

Knight of Labor   £48

L

Landlord in Love, The   £110

Lady of 1865 and Dandy of 1865
each; £15

Landlord in Love, The   £110

Landlord in Love, The   £180

The reverse side depicts a young lady
seated at a table with an oil lamp on it.

Last in Bed To Put Out the Light, The
£6

Last in Bed To Put Out The Light, The
£8

Let Us Do Business Together   £20

Last Match, The   £28
(Also captioned 'Pat's Last Match')

Let Us Speak of a Man as we Find Him
£620

Let Us Be Friends   £25

Little Bo Peep   £14

Little Boy Blue £14

Little Shoemaker, The £280

Little John in Trouble £15

Little Turk, A £11

Little Red Riding Hood £14

Liverpool to Menai Bridge £20

Long Pull and a Strong Pull £120

Looking Down Upon His Luck £45

Looking Down Upon His Luck £55

Looking Out (the pair)£20

Looking Down Upon His Luck £22

Lor Three Legs! I'll Charge 2d. £25

Lor Three Legs! I'll Charge 2d. £30

Lost £50

Lor Three Legs! I'll Charge 2d. £60

Love on the Tiles £20

Lor Three Legs! I'll Charge 2d £75

Lovers Disturbed, The £200

Love's First Lesson £22

Girl teaching boy to knit a sock

Low Life £28

Lucky Dog, A £30
(Also captioned 'Privileged Pet, A')

 M

Mama £10

Many Happy Returns £5

Manx Cat £25

Married for Money £30

Masters Winning Ways £300

Married Blessedness £28

Match, Sir £70
(Also Captioned 'Any Lights Sir')

Midnight's Holy Hour £35

Missus is Master £32

Model of Laxey, The £12

Modesty £55

Montague Tigg £20

Morning Prayer £21

Morning Prayer £21
(Properly captioned 'Evening Prayer')

Mr. Jones Take off Your Hat £60

Mouse! Mouse! £40

Mr. Micawber £10

Mr. Jones Remove Your Hat £80

Mr. Micawber Conducts David Home £12

56

Mr. Moody   £10

Mr. Sankey   £10

Mr. Pecksniff   £10

Much Ado About Nothing   £20

Murder, The   £55

Music Hath Charms £35

Mylord and Milady £50

My Old Country Seat £5

N

Naughty Words £50

Necessity Knows No Law £20

New Woman, The   £40

New York to Boston
Pinbox and matchstriker.   £16

Nice Views   £220

Night Before Christmas, The   £95

Night Cap, The   £40

Nip on the Sly, A   £40

No Followers Allowed   £320

Nothing Ventured, Nothing Have!
Mother holding up girl, child reaching
up. Very rare. Price negotiable but
unlikely to be less than   £250

Now Dogs, Jump £40

Now Ma'rm, Say When? £40

Now I'm Grandmama £10 Now They'll Blame Me For This £45

Off to the Seaside   £13

Oh Do Leave Me a Drop   £75

Off to the Seaside   £13

Oh What a Difference in the Morning
£50

Oft in the Stilly Night   £40

Old Welsh Spinning Wheel, The   £10

One O'Clock in the Morning   £25

Open Your Mouth and Shut Your Eyes

£300

One O'Clock in the Morning   £25

Opportunity Creates Thieves   £20

Organ Boy, The   £290

On the Rink   £100

Orphans, The   £40

Our Best Wishes £250

Orphans, The £40

Our Best Wishes £230

Our Lodger's Such a Nice Young Man
£60

Ornament Fire Stove £60

Oyster Day   **£50**

Our Snappish Mother-In-Law   **£40**

Our Soldiers   **£90**

Oysters Sir?   **£30**

Ou Sont Les Rats   **£75**

Out! By Jingo!   **£400**   **Oysters Sir?**   **£45**

P

Paddling His Own Canoe £15

Pastoral Visit By Rev. John Jones, A
£15

Pat's Last Match £28

Peau D'Lapin Chiffons

A boy carrying a dead rabbit in his hand. £26

Papa £10

Peep Through Telescope, A £15

Please Sir What Would You Charge To Christen My Doll? £150

Pins Madame? £25

Pluck £40

Pleasant Termination To a Happy Evening, A £260

Polen Abschied £74

Polly and Scotch   £12

Power of Love, The   £35

Present from Canterbury   £10

Present From Canterbury   £10

Present from Cricieth   £10

Present From Criccieth   £10

Present From Dalmuir

Groups of children with animals.   £10

Present From North Wales   **£8**

A match striker.

Present from Rhyl   **£15**

Prince of Wales   **£8**

Present from Torquay   **£10**

Prince of Wales

Edward VII as a small boy in a sailor suit standing beside a tub.   **£8**

Priviledged Pet, A   **£30**
(Also captioned 'A Lucky Dog')

Quiet Interruption   (Also captioned 'I Will Warm You')   **£320**

Ready to Start   **£10**   **Ready to Start**   **£10**

**Reception At Three O'Clock in the
Morning** £15

Rent in Arrear £35
Rent Settled £35

Girl putting patch in trousers of a man

Return from the Ball £90

Retour de Voyage
Very rare and unrecorded at auction
Price subject to negotiation but un-
likely to be less than £400

**Returning at One O'Clock in the
Morning** £25

Return, The £290

**Returning at One O'Clock in the
Morning** £18

Returning From Journey
Very rare and unrecorded at auction. Price subject to negotiation but unlikely to be less than **£400**

Returning From Working
Square-based matchstriker showing a little boy carrying a shovel **£42**

Revu **£785**

Rip Van Winkle **£18**

Robbing The (Male) Mail **£45**

Rough on Boys **£15**

Royal Manchester Exchange **£10**

Rub A Dub Dub Three Men in a Tub **£5**

Safe Messenger, A £20

Seeing Him Home £170

Shakespeare's Courtship £40

Sarah's Young Man £38

Sedan £320

Shall We sleep First or How? £22

Shamming Sick £75

She Had What She Wanted and Leaves the Inn £410

**Sir! Where's Your Gloves?
If You Think To Go Out With Me £300**

Shoemaker In Love, The £250

Six Mois Apres La Noce £22

Sir Francis Drake £10

Slack £80

Sleeping Beauty   £60

Souter Johannie
Tam O'Shanter   £14

Soft Repose   £300

Spicy Bit, A   £42

Some Contributors to Punch   £240

Spoils of War, The   £35

Stop Your Tickling Jock £45

Swansea to Bristol £18

Sturm Schewerer Cavallerie £50

Sweet Song (Love's Old) £40

Surprise, The £294
(Also Captioned 'Wet Reception')

Sweet Violets Sir £75

Swell, A £50

Sympathy £189

Taking a Walk £9

Taking Dessert
A woman caresses a man kneeling by
her side. Very rare and unrecorded
at auction. Price subject to negotiation. Unlikely to be less than **£500**

Tea Party £35

Taking the Cream £55

10,000 £8

That's Funny, Very Funny!
Very Very Funny! £48

Three O'Clock in the Morning £10

Three O'Clock in the Morning £24

Three's None

Sold with Two's Company. £42

Times, The £8

The Pet £15

To Epsom £700 - £1,400

Tom Pouce £60

To Epsom £400 - £800

Top Slice, The (Fake caption) £30

To Let £300

Trespassing £140

Triple Alliance £15

Twelve Months After Marriage £30

Truly Any Form Is Not Evil £105

Tug of War £35

Twelve Months After Marriage £20

Tug of War £40

Twelve Months After Marriage £20

Twelve Months After Marriage   £15

Two Different Views (Front)   £900

Two Different Views   £180

Two Different Views (Back)   £900

 U

Under Petticoat Government   £40

Une Heure Monsieur   £25

Une Mauvaise Rencontre £400

United We Stand, Divided We Fall £50

Union For Ever £15

Unser Fritz £380

Velocipede For Stout Travellers £550

Victoire, La £35

Velocipeding on a Rainy Day £1,100

Very Much Frightened £20

Vy Sarah You're Drunk £50

W

Walk In   **£400**

Waiting For a Bus   **£300**

Walk In Please   **£180**

Waiting For Orders   **£20**

Wedding Night, The   **£25**
(Clock missing)

Wedding Night, The £30

Welsh Costume. £10

Well! What Are You Looking At?
£340

Welsh Costume £25

Welsh Spinning Party £5

Welsh Tea Party, The £16

Welsh Tea Party, The £16

Welsh Tea Party, The £16

Welsh Tea Party, The £8

Welsh Tea Party, The £20

Welsh Tea Party, The £20

Welsh Tea Party, The £16

Welsh Tea Party, The £8

Wendas Alter Konte £15

What Have These Met For? £300

Wet Reception, The £294

What Have These Met For? £300

We Won't Go Home Till Morning
£32

What is Home Without a Mother - In - Law? £38

What Peace When the Old Girl Sleeps
£20

What Peace When the Old Girl Sleeps
£25

When A Man's Married His Troubles Begin
£12

When a Man is Married His Troubles Begin
£28

When Mother's At the Wash
£70

Where Are You Going To My Pretty Maid?
£50

Which is the Prettiest? £28
(Also captioned 'Quelle est la Plus
Belle') £35

Who is Coming? £65

Who Said Rats? £65

Who Calls! £120

Who Calls? £120

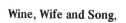

Wine, Wife and Song, £300

You Dirty Boy £12

You Naughty Boy £20

You Dirty Girl £20

Young Cups and Old Cups £30

Uncaptioned Fairings

All Over   £50

If You Please Sir   £100

Benoni and Leila   £10

Chess Players, The   £25   Mr. Micawber   £10

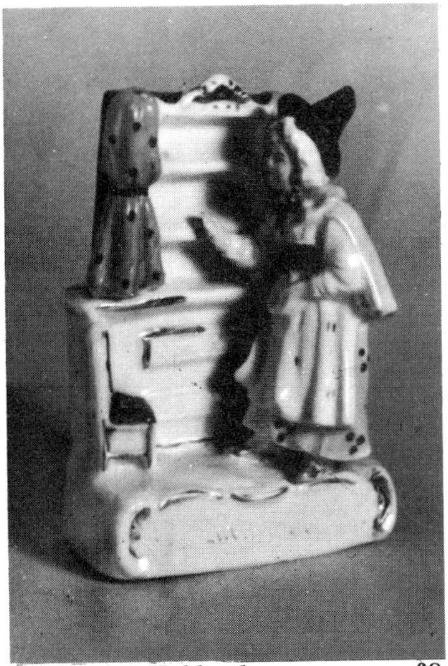

Old Mother Hubbard £8

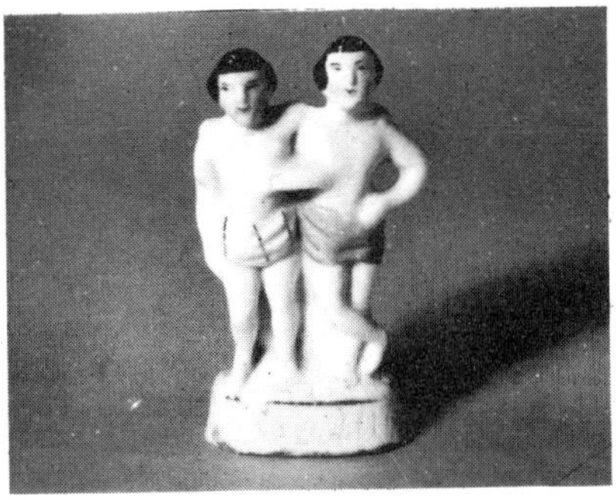

Siamese Twins £35

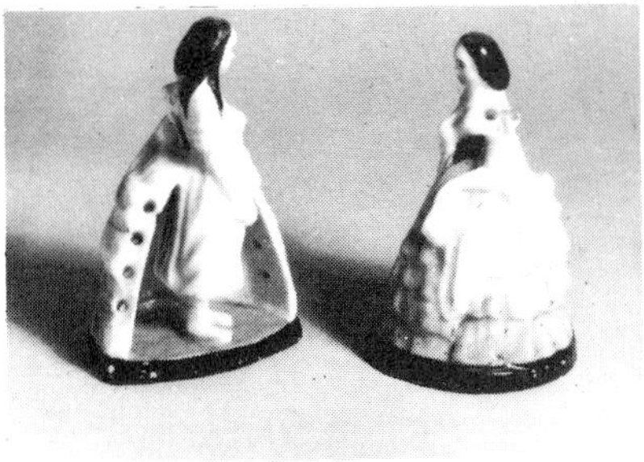

Queen Victoria and Plain Jane £45

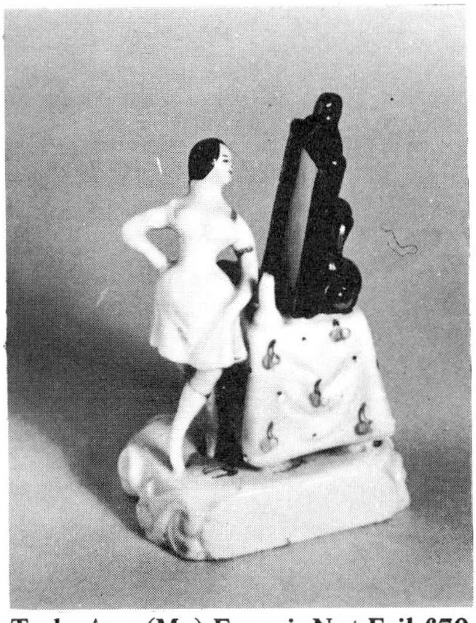

Truly Any (My) Form is Not Evil £70

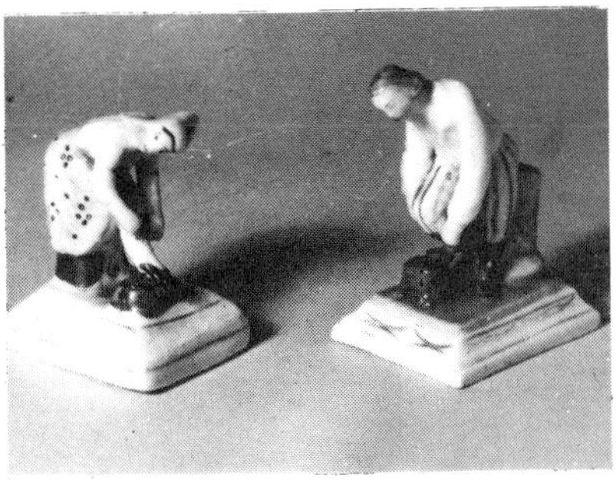

Search, The Each £20

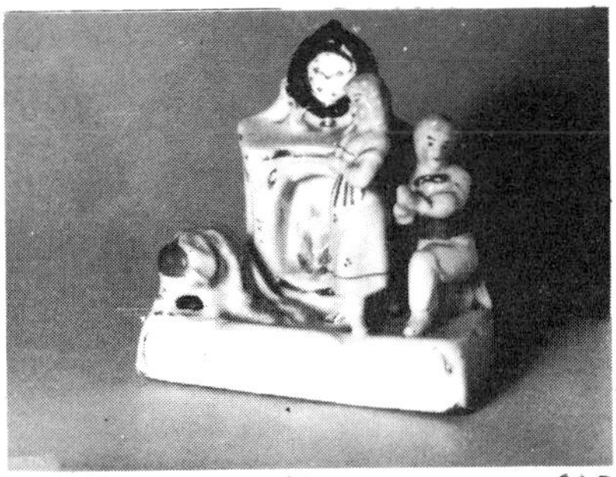

Wedding Night, The £15

`Brothel´
Series

£25

Figure (left)   £15
Figure (right)   £10

£15

£10

£20

£40

Each figure **£15**

`Vienna´ Series

£300

£290

The Vienna Series consists of five pieces made at the Royal Vienna Factory in about 1860. The fifth figure (unillustrated) is very rare and depicts a man in the bath with a woman entering the room.

Distinguishing features of this series are their mitred bases with a broad gilt central band and an impressed gilded line below the top edge.

£400

£400

Untitled Fairings

£16

£100

£15

£25

£12

£6

£4

£10

£8

£25

£8

£20

£30

£15

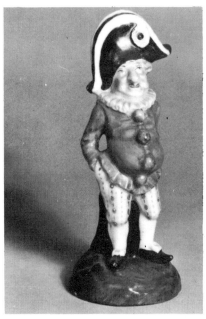

£16

£20

£5

£10

£30

£100

£30

99

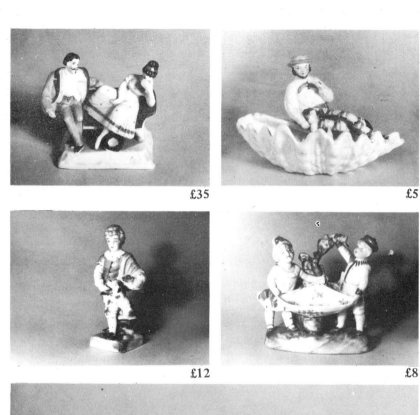

£35

£5

£12

£8

£20

Match Holders and Strikers

£26

£6

£10

£8

£5

£10

£8

£5

£5

£5

£6

£6

£5

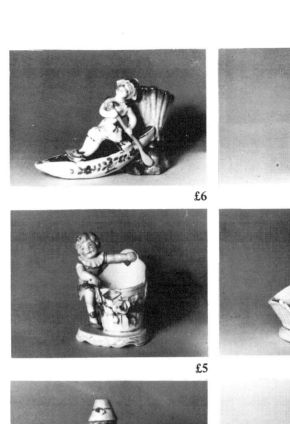

£5

£5

£5

£5

£5

£5

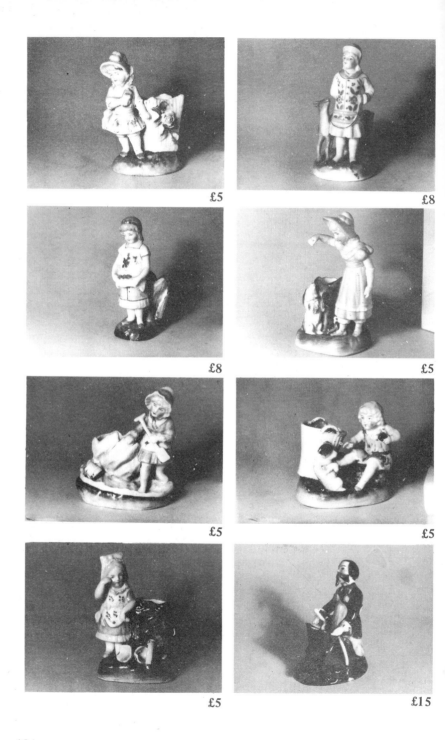

£5

£8

£8

£5

£5

£5

£5

£15

£10

£8

£8

£5

£5

£5

£8

£5

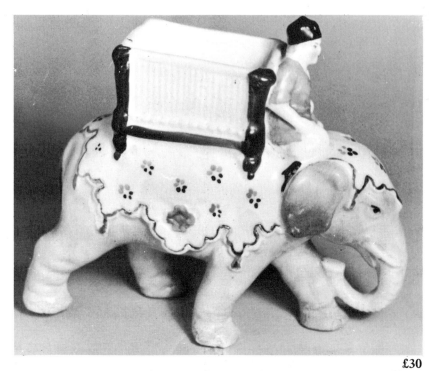

£30

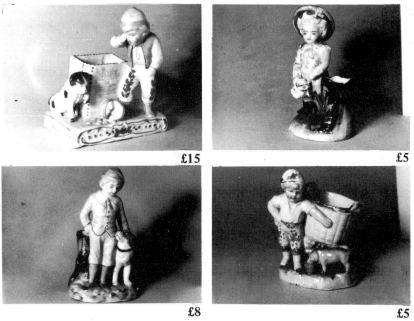

£15

£5

£8

£5

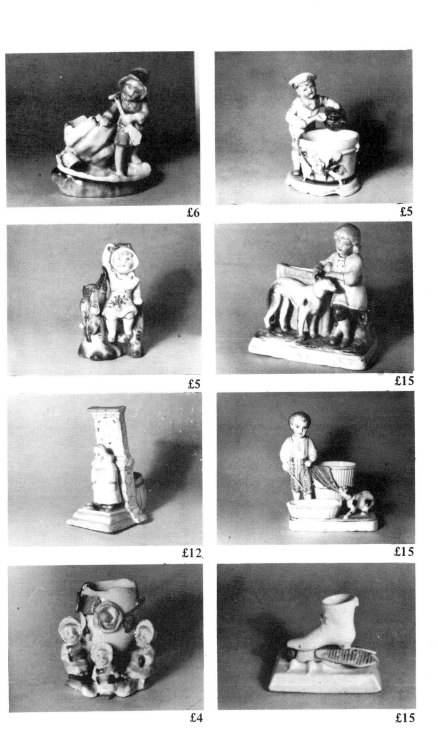

£6

£5

£5

£15

£12

£15

£4

£15

Pin Boxes

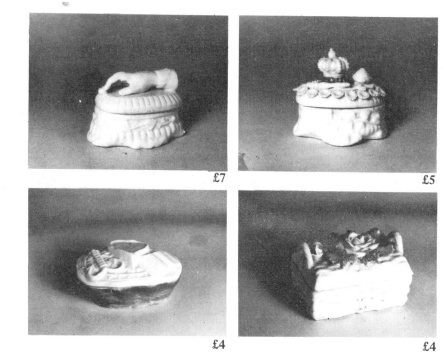

£7

£5

£4

£4

£8

£3

£4

£5

£4

£4

£5

£3

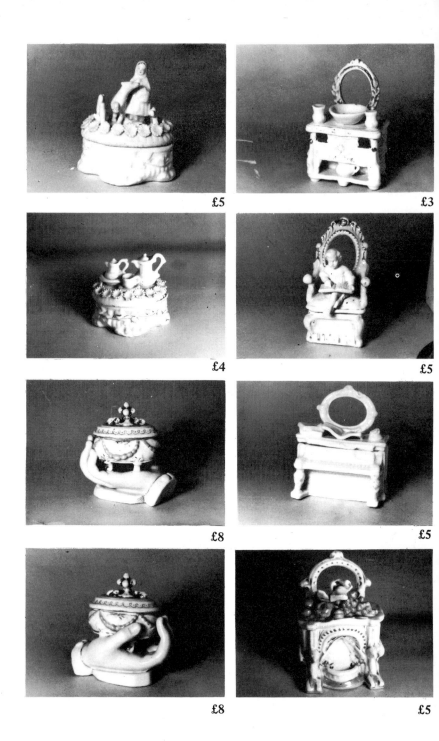

£5

£3

£4

£5

£8

£5

£8

£5

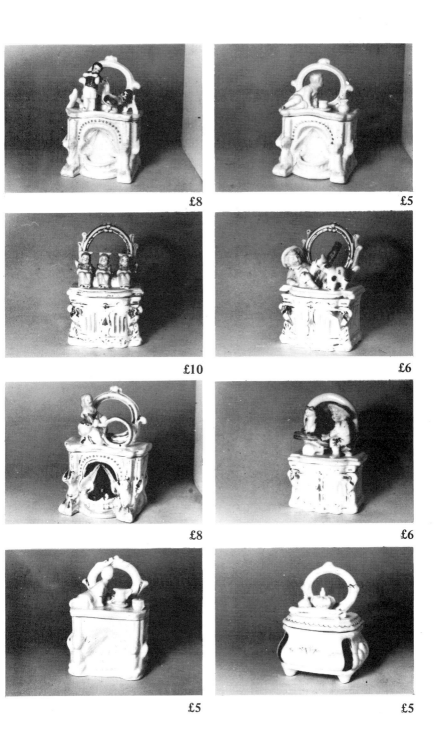

£8

£5

£10

£6

£8

£6

£5

£5

111

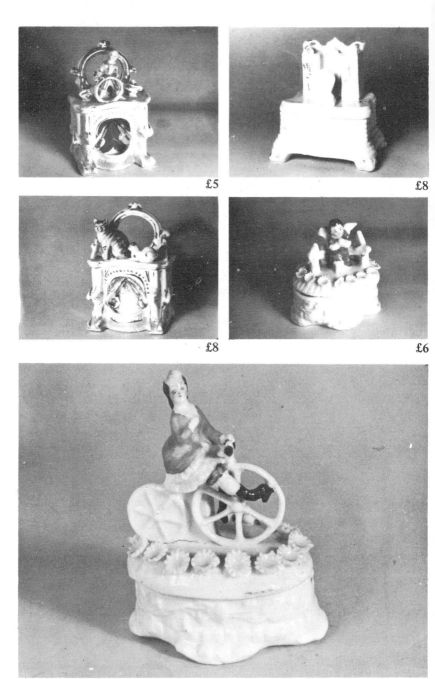

£5

£8

£8

£6

£30

£20

£6

£8

£5

£10

£10

£12

£10

£10

£10

£15

£6

£5

£12   £15

£15   £10

£20

£10

£15

£10

£4

£20

£4

£8

£4

£8

£6

£15

£12

£5

117

£8

£8

£12

£12

£5

£4

£8

£12

£10

left £5 right £20

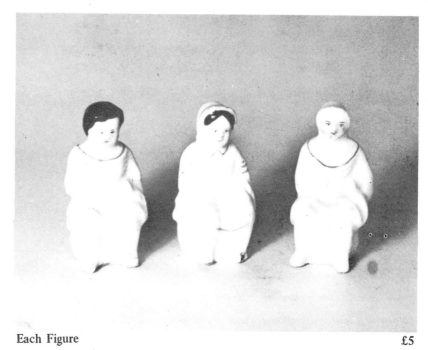

Each Figure £5

£4

£12

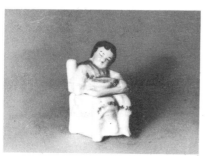

£4

£20

INDEX